The Legend of the Kettle Daughter

First published 2019 by The Hedgehog Poetry Press

Published in the UK by
The Hedgehog Poetry Press, 5 Coppack House, Churchill Avenue, Clevedon
BS21 6QW

www.hedgehogpress.co.uk

ISBN: 978-1-9164806-5-0

Copyright © Amy Alexander 2019

The right of Amy Alexander to be identified as the author of this work has been asserted by her in accordance with the Copyright, Designs and Patents Act 1988.

All artwork © Amy Alexander

All rights reserved. No part of this publication may be reproduced, stored in or introduced into a retrieval system, or transmitted in any form, or by any means (electronic, mechanical, photocopying, recording or otherwise) without prior written permissions of the publisher. Any person who does any unauthorised act in relation to this publication may be liable for criminal prosecution and civil claims for damages,

9 8 7 6 5 4 3 2 1

A CIP Catalogue record for this book is available from the British Library.

The Legend of the Kettle Daughter

by

Amy Alexander

Contents

- Birth of the Kettle Daughter 9
- Silver passed To Kettle Daughter 11
- Kettle Daughter Finds Stories 13
- Kettle Daughter In Winter 15
- Kettle Daughter In School 17
- Kettle Daughter Lives twice 19
- Red Kettle Daughter Days 21
- Kettle Daughter Has A Vision 23
- Kettle Daughter's Daughter Is Born 25
- Kettle Daughter's Wish 27
- The Joyful Era Of The Kettle Daughter 29
- Kettle Daughter's Star Song 31
- The Coming Of The Second Kettle Daughter 33
- Kettle Daughter Grows More Distant 35
- The Dying Of The Kettle Daughter 37

My mother grew up in Salt Lake City, Utah, and spent summers at her grandfather's cabin in a place known as Holiday Park, near the headwaters of the Weber River, in the Wasatch Mountains. Her father also spent his childhood there. When she was 21, she left Utah, and moved to Denver, Colorado.

Throughout my childhood, she spoke of her upbringing with mythic language. Time in the mountains and in Salt Lake City became tinged with a kind of shimmering distance that seemed to reach back hundreds of years, rather than a couple of decades. We visited my great grandfather's cabin frequently, and she wove her stories in, around bonfires as tall as the sky. It added to her mysticism.

As I grew, my relationship with these stories shifted. I found that my mother was plagued as a girl with seasons of deep emotional pain. This tinged my childhood, too, because my mother was often very absorbed in healing from childhood wounds. As a psychiatric nurse, she was an expert in helping others unravel their own emotional pain.

When my mother was reaching the end of her life, after breast cancer had metastasized, she wanted to go back to Utah. I went there, too, to help her die. In those painful weeks, the things I had imagined about her life before I came along blended with the sometimes painful truth about my Mormon ancestors that explained why my mother left, eagerly, as soon as she could.

I stayed in the Salt Lake City area for a time after my mother died, and got a chance to return to the family's Holiday Park summer cabin. There, I felt the thick grief of losing my mother lift. She returned, for me, to the mythological landscape where I had placed her as a child, listening to her stories.

I dedicate this poetry and artwork to Barbara Pratt Reynolds (1943-2015), who is now flying above the mountains, and to my daughter, Charlotte, the second kettle daughter, who was born healthy, despite the fact that she was compromised by a blood clot while in the womb. I also wish to acknowledge the presence of the wonderful men in my life, my father, Sam, my husband, David, and my son, Ryan, who made me a mom, the greatest gift of all.

Birth of the Kettle Daughter

There is iron here,
in the rocks
and in the veins.
It is under the water,
painted by fish shadows
and fire at night
and in the daughter.

Clot children are born
in the kitchen,
the kettle cried
and blood turned to girl,

at least it seemed like that
to the soldier
who named her after
strangers.

He had to wait to bring her to the woods,
and war months last years,
so it was decades.

He was afraid
she would have lost
her wildness,
shaking all the time,
he held her,
waded to cross the
water into the forest
of his fathers.

Silver passed To Kettle Daughter

Her mother brought the silver down
and prepared her a place.

Teaspoons measure out
the honey collected
from Brigham's bee boxes,
mother to daughter,
the wedding gift goes hand to hand
like that,
but what is passed isn't etched with calligraphy
but in the bones,

ear drums catch the song
so it can be repeated
at birthdays and beside last breath beds,
not always sung well,
but repeated, still,
and still and still,
the things we know
without having to write them down.

Kettle Daughter Finds Stories

By five,
she could travel, blindfolded,
to the bowl of light
known as Yellow Lake.
Kettle boys kill,
first mice,
then badgers,
make a winter skin,
deer and goat,
mountain lion,
buffalo to eat.
Kettle daughter
finds stories,
small scenes
to epic poems,
braided plots
reveal meaning.
At Henrietta Falls,
where Yellow Lake
roars into darkness,
she breathed creatures
into the grassy mist.
The cloven-hooved
grew bold and came to listen,
the bears heeded.

Trees gained magic
and lived three times longer.
She told the other children
to look for things
in the hollows,
pennies, bottle caps, feathers,
felt hats,
fossilized fish
no longer found
in these parts
of the cold spring.

Kettle Daughter In Winter

In the city of salt,
kettle daughter fit into a box.
This took strain,
fold into the city,
expand into woods, again.

Winter filling valley,
a frozen yard,
Father and Mother
sliding circles under stars.

She was supposed to sleep
but watched, sky and ice skaters,
heated hands under sodden wool.

Her breath on glass,
tracing the outline of trees,
woods calling from the high country,
cabin under 25 feet of snow,
tree trunk bracing the roof,
slender snowflakes pressing
on the creaking nails laid by her grandfather.

Kettle Daughter In School

Every classmate had a country inside,
and her mind captured it.

Kettle Daughter walked the width
of a schoolyard
to befriend distance,
children whose skin stung
in the city of salt,
who couldn't be trusted,
spent Sundays
in the green cathedral,
chanted the mass
or knelt in unfamiliar ways.

In the land of outcasts,
castaways become masters
at shunning,
and Kettle Daughter,
born of the world's blood,
felt rent at the center for each one,
sang all their histories
wore their geographies
across her back.

Kettle Daughter Lives twice

Kettle Daughter learns women's ways at an early age.
She is elder to the children in her house,
carries them across the yard
and breaks away with them on the back of her bike.

They taste air and cry wind,
they touch desert
and do not know the number of canyon blasts
she catches with her body.

At 12, she trades in the care market,
pockets dollars
for mystery stories.

She feels too ordinary,
then come the days
she knows she is made
of something else,
both an everyday Nancy Drew
and the hidden staircases,
haunted bridges
and wild horses told
in tales by night.

Red Kettle Daughter Days

Kettle Daughter's amulets,
plain and strange,
in a girl's papyrus and purse,
shoes she donned and longed for
and coiffes
drawn in the margins
of her journal,
with pages sliced out,
pins and slips of paper,
collected lipsticks,
all of them fire.

At Saltair Pavilion,
she reeled into the lights
on an ancient roller coaster,
drank Coca-Cola,
grew sick,
hid evidence
in the folds of her green sack.

There were many things
she told no one,
writing them, instead,

A beloved auntie returns
from across the plains
as an uncle
takes his last breaths,
in concert, on her pages,
goodbye in blood ink

Kettle Daughter Has A Vision

Measles drum
on her sweaty head
and it's another Halloween.

In the dark valley,
fabric spectres trace
up and down straight streets,
fire shapes counting
North and South,
East and West,
addresses numbered up from the Temple,
its corner stone
set down
by grandfather's father.

She doesn't exactly know,
but she somehow remembers
unspoken rituals, unsaintly,
older than rocks.

Kettle Daughter's Daughter Is Born

Kettle Daughter's story to her children
started late,
in a plastic suitcase
leaving behind the city of salt
and the cabin in the woods.

We pictured her floating,
snagged downriver
by a rock set on a shrine.

In the dirty city,
mile high,
they tipped strong drink
into teacups,
cooled it with snow
scraped from skis.

Kettle daughter's hand rattled,
she married the man who steadied them.

I came along.
Not a kettle daughter,
no clot origin
or wild animals,
just brushes for painting.

I existed, an audience,
as she spoke everything
into myth,
every person she met
was folded into her,
heated to life by words
in a line I could follow,
her belly to mine,
our faces just enough alike.

Kettle Daughter's Wish

Kettle Daughter's wish
was to heal minds.
She wanted to help hurt children,
and so they were flung to her,
by stars.

The world bruised us, too,
but being born of a Kettle Daughter
makes you stronger than others,
so was her mantra.

We put on metal smiles.
We radiated joy
and saved our sorrows,
histories, instead of fortunes,
on tiny scraps of paper
under our pillows.

When we grew up,
we had things to say
around campfires.

The Joyful Era Of The Kettle Daughter

Kettle Daughter moves to the water
called *Yampah* by the old people.
Some of the families, here,
live in caves.
Others bathe there,
hissing rocks
give voice to shifting vapors,
whispered chants without words,
unknown, now, to all
is the neverending cave maze.
We feel it with our feet.

Kettle Daughter recognizes the rhythm of it
and dances.
This is her joy season,
snow swallows sun
in big gulps
as the hours vanish,
winter days flash, quick,
like flint,
before the dusk moves in,
then runoff to spring
and summers.

When she is called home
to the Weber's head waters,
she goes there,
looks at herself
reflected in Yellow Lake,
speckled trout sisters
swimming across her face

Kettle Daughter's Star Song

She of a full-throated trill
in the autumn of her life
is called the Star Lady
and sings
beneath constellations.

I cannot learn the words to her song.

They stop in my throat,
and though I tell her tales,
and bring my friends to her planetarium
where she plays Zepplin's Kashmere
and sets the stars reeling,
I cannot quite speak to her,
and she can't grasp my poetry.

She paints the trees around Henrietta Falls
while I put souls down
on cotton paper and can't see green
the way the Kettle Daughters do.

The Coming Of The Second Kettle Daughter

The baby's first picture
is a song,
sound bounced around
etches an image
lights a room like fire
from the cabin stove,
hauled up to the headwaters
in pieces.

At first, gasping,
there were two.
And then we saw
this was a clot,
unwelcome stranger
marked my girl a miracle
and made her a kettle daughter, too.

Though not one myself,
I recognize the burden.

She will live each event
more than the rest.
She will taste the iron of stars,
recognize rocks,
carry stories.

Kettle Daughter Grows More Distant

Kettle Daughter spoke a second language
to slow down her visions.
Wandering the streets,
she fed the hungry
then joined them.

Calling from the foot of the monument,
beside the rock animals
and painted handprints,
above the sprinkler farms
and sweet orchards,
her voice was a tin cymbal
I couldn't answer.

Grandfather twirls floss in the sky
seeking fish,
her own body,
a girl then,
in solstice light that never stops,
flying toward midnight,
St. Elmo's Fire,
an octopus reaching toward stars,
her father talking to the light people,
then wondering if they were really there.

The Dying Of The Kettle Daughter

Twenty-one days
before going,
Kettle Daughter refused
to discuss the details
of the Undiscovered Country.

Moonlight Sonata
was brought in to drown out
bombs splitting the sky
and rattles,
the rise and fall
of her turning into wind.

A year later,
I stopped by the spring at Yellow Lake.
The water spoke
and the trees whispered.

Down the trail to Henrietta Falls,
Kettle Daughter's call
sounded like Owl.

www.ingramcontent.com/pod-product-compliance
Lightning Source LLC
Chambersburg PA
CBHW040014080526
44586CB00028B/3001